SAP PM Interview Questions, Answers, and Explanations

SAPCOOKBOOK.COM

Please visit our website at www.sapcookbook.com

ISBN 1-933804-13-0

TABLE OF CONTENTS

SAP PM Interview Questions, Answers, and Explanations

SAPCOOKBOOK
Equity Press

☞ QUESTION 1

DP90 change invoices quantity via DIP profile

We use DP90 resource related billing to bill our service orders and transfer the actual cost to a pricing condition in the sales debit note request.

We then change the proposed percentage rate in the dip profile (source) to 115% -> and add a surcharge of 15% (or 30% depending on situation) in the DP90 overview, the initial quantity, initial amount, quantity to be billed, and amount to be billed are correctly shown. Our problem is the quantity in the SD order. We would like the initial quantity to be used with the calculated new price, but SAP seem to transfer only the calculated new quantity and initial price and use SD pricing functionality to determine the net price.

For example:

1 PC - 100 EUR -> surcharge of 10 % -> 110 EUR

The result in SD is as follows:

QTY: 1, 1 PC Base Price 100 EUR Total Price 110 EUR;

Is there anyone who knows if this can be customized?

Can user exit be used to influence the configuration and results?

A second problem that we have is that when we cancel the debit note request and redo RRB with DP90 the system uses the recalculated quantity and the price as starting point, and adds another time to the surcharge.

For example: 2nd DP90 qty = 1, 1 pc* 1.10 and price = 121 EUR;

Depending on the selection criteria of the DIP profile, we have also proposed percentage 115% or 130%. In one sales order, there can be items with 115%, other with 130%.

Labor costs: 100 EUR -> surcharge 115 EUR for 1.15 H;
Material: 10 EUR -> surcharge 130 EUR of 1.30PC;

On the invoice we want 1 h for 115 EUR and 1 PC for 130 EUR instead of 1, 15 h and 1.30 pc;

How can we fix this?

✍ ANSWER

The "usual" method used for this process is the accounting indicator.

In the service order header you will see a two-digit field called accounting indicator (Accounting Indicator). The field can also be seen in confirmation documents (IW41) and (DP90).

With this field you can set discounts/surcharges. You can also use condition type KMB1 (or is it KBM1) in conjunction with accounting indicators.

As standard, the accounting indicator is copied from the service order header to the DP90 screen, or via confirmation documents.

If this is not happening in your system, then check any RRB user-exits (AD01*) or OSS for a relevant note.

☞ Question 2

Regarding Call Horizon in the Maintenance Plan

If we create a Maintenance Plan with reference to a Package which has different cycles say (Weekly, Monthly, and Yearly). The call horizon is applied based on the least frequency.

For example:

If the call date is calculated as 3 days earlier for a Weekly cycle, it holds good for the monthly and Yearly cycle.

My client wants a different call horizon for each cycle defined in the Maintenance Package.

Is there any way to configure it as required by the client?

✍ Answer

This is standard functionality. You can utilize user-exits to change these values.

☞ QUESTION 3

Date used for Maintenance Plan Scheduling using Shift Factor

I need some confirmation information on Maintenance Plan Scheduling.

If you are using maintenance plan and makes use of Shift Factors, what date is used in the adjustment of the maintenance Plan which is considering previous order?

Is it the TECO date on the Order or is it on the Confirmations date?

I have heard it is on the first confirmed operation but cannot believe this, unless it is adjusted with every sub-sequent confirmation.

I do not have access to a system currently. Is there an explanation on the written principle to Plan Adjustments when using Shift Factors?

✍ ANSWER

You know that really annoying pop-up box that appears when you TECO and order? The one with the reference date and time?

This is the information used as a basis for the shift factors.

In the newer versions, there are two reference dates and times. One of them is specifically used for maintenance plans.

The new functionality is available from version 4.7 onwards. You need to activate this for each of the maintenance plan category.

☞ QUESTION 4

Copy Functional location

I need to transfer the FL and EQ.

Can we copy a functional location with its equipments from one plant to another plant? If so, then what do we need in the target plant?

✍ ANSWER

You can copy the FLoc structure via TCode IL04; however you cannot copy the equipment.

At first, create in the customizing all the objects depending on planning and maintenance plant: Company area, planer group, and location.

Than, create the new work center, and cost center for the new plant.

Download, from the functional location, all the data depending on planning and the maintenance plant.

Do the same for the pieces of equipment if they are not installed on functional location.

At the first level of the FL, change the maintenance plant. Normally, the system changes all the data on all the sub level and EQ. Now you can reload on FL and/or EQ all the data depending on planning and maintenance plant.

☞ QUESTION 5

Maintenance Order-TECO

I have created a Purchase Requisition through a Maintenance Order by using Non-stock item category. Later, I decided that I don't want that material for that work. So I ticked on Clear Reservation at the time of Confirmation in IW42. When I tried to Tech the Maintenance Order, I am getting the following error message:

"Final issue for the reservation item 0001 is not completed, teco not possible Message no. ME303"

How can I do Tech without the need of that material?

I won't create a PO normally if I do Clear Reservation at the time of confirmation. Automatically, the system will delete the PR. It's happening in IDES.

It didn't happen in Production server (ECC 5.0) though.

How can I do Tech without the need of that material?

✍ ANSWER

It sounds very much like a User Exit (Enhancement) may be active in your system. The TECO User Exit to consider is: IWO10004.

Use Transaction CMOD so you can see if there is such an exit possible.

Drop down on the project field to search for a project associated with indicated exit. Search by “Information System” and at the bottom of the selection screen there is an Icon called “All Selections” [Shows a little + sign too].

Now once you have expanded the selection criteria insert the indicated User Exit Number in the “Enhancement” field. Execute and wait to see if there is a project associated with the exit at TECO. If there is one, select it and select the DISPLAY ICON.

Once the data is shown there is a “Project Status”. If this is “Active”, then you have an active exit on TECO.

I suggest you have an ABAPer look at the code associated in the “Include” of the exit.

I suspect there is code checking a flag on the Materials or something.

☞ QUESTION 6

Deletion Flag for a FL

Even when we have set a Deletion flag for a Functional Location, it allows us to install Equipment in it. Our requirement is that the System should disallow it.

Is it a standard functionality of SAP?

✍ ANSWER

Yes it is.

This could be blocked by using a user status.

☞ Question 7

Copy of functional location

I have a requirement from a client that he wants to copy the Functional location with its equipment from one plant to another plant if it is possible.

If yes, how can I accomplish this?

✍ Answer

Try transaction cc04:

- Use a filter to display only what you need in the hierarchy;
- From the hierarchy display, right mouse click on the node you need to copy;
- From the context options dialog, select 'Copy sub hierarchy';

Test this thoroughly before using in your Production system as it is possible to create part of your structure. If SAP encounters a problem with an object, the rest of the structure will not be created.

☞ QUESTION 8

Accounting Indicator in DP91

The accounting indicator entered in the header of the service order applies to all labor and parts confirmed and issued. We see the accounting indicator when we do DP91. If we change the accounting indicator from say 01 (billable) to 03 (warranty) this transfers into the repair order (seen on the sales b tab), but the costs still post to 01.

Why do the costs not repost to the correct accounts based on the accounting indicator in DP91?

✍ ANSWER

Check your pricing procedure to see what account key (ActKy) is set for the condition type (the standard is KBM1). From there, you can proceed to correct any errors.

☞ Question 9

Maintenance Plan User Status

I can create a profile available to Maintenance Plans. However, I am not able to allocate it.

Is it possible to assign a user status to a Maintenance Plan?

✍ Answer

In the 47 system, you can assign the user-status to a maintenance plan.

Please check ECC5 or ECC6 for verification of profile data.

☞ QUESTION 10

Identify parts as billable or non-billable

We need to identify parts in the service order as billable or non-billable. We are using the accounting indicator on the header of the service order to identify warranty or non-warranty repair. However, entering the accounting indicator here applies to all parts and labor confirmed and issued to the service order. We want to be able to enter an accounting indicator or some other process of identifying individual parts as billable or non-billable.

✍ ANSWER

You can enter the accounting indicator in DP90 instead.

☞ Question 11

User defined fields in list editing

When we do enhancement by adding user defined fields in notification is it possible to select notifications based on user defined fields in list editing transaction?

✍ Answer

My guess is that you will not be able to see the customer-specific fields in the standard list edit programs.

But you can simply copy these programs and include the fields yourself.

☞ Question 12

External repair

We are trying to do In-house repair process and we are using SM03 order type to create the RAS order. This process is okay and running smooth.

Now there is new requirement, the guys here does not repair all the equipments in-house. Some are sent to vendors for repair and I tried using the SM03 control key and I am able to key in a GL account and able to generate a Preq.

When I try to convert this Preq into a Po the system gives me an error message saying that, "The service order cannot carry revenues". See the detailed message below.

Since this is a RAS order and we are using the std SM03 service order which is not relevant for revenue posting.

May be I am missing something here, Can some one guide me here?

The message:

Order 4124749 cannot carry revenues
Message no. KO 014

Diagnosis
You have tried to post an order, which is not allowed to carry revenues, under a revenue element (or the system determined the order automatically).

The field "Revenues" in the order type determines whether

revenues can be posted to an order or not. Orders carrying revenues cannot be settled to a cost center.

System Response
Order 4124749 cannot carry revenues.

Procedure
You can either

enter a different order.
enter a different cost element (not a revenue element).

✍ ANSWER

What cost element are you using?

It looks like the service master(s) are picking-up a revenue element when it should be a cost element!!

Check with your FI/CO team

☞ QUESTION 13

Notification and orders across planning plants

Is it possible to have a notification created for planning plant A, then create a service order for planning plant B for that notification? From there, is it also possible to create a res. rel. billing document for that service order in the sales organization assigned to planning plant A?

This is the current set-up:

Notification - created in plant A;
Service order - created in plant B;
Rec. rel. billing document - created in sales org assigned to plant A;

The problem is that plant A and the sales organization belongs to company code A but plant B belongs to company code B.

How do we go about cross planning?

✍ ANSWER

I don't see how. Plant A and Plant B and the Sales Organization exist with a different Company Code.

This constitutes inter-company trading.

You will need to consult with your FI/CO team.

☞ QUESTION 14

Catalogs in PM order / Task List

What is the purpose of Catalog tab in Task List and PM order?

I find this in the component overview of orders and task lists. We maintained BOMs for equipment. We use catalogs for Notification.

How to use catalogs in the component overview of order?

Do we need to do some settings in material master?

✍ ANSWER

If you are referring to the Catalog button at the bottom of the Components tab, then this is used to link to an internal/ external internet site where you can order spare parts.

Have a look in the PM IMG for OCI (under orders).

☞ QUESTION 15

Catalog profile for Equipment

What is the process for maintaining catalog a profile for each equipment?

We have a general catalog profile for all the equipment. We are interested in having a display of catalogs for the selected equipment in Notifications.

Is it possible to maintain catalog profiles for Functional locations?

✍ ANSWER

Create a catalog profile and assign it to your equipment in the Organization tab. This will then be copied to the Notification when the equipment number is entered.

The same works for Functional locations.

☞ QUESTION 16

Actual variance maintenance plan

In Maintenance plan we get the Actual variance (of Day) in "maintenance plan schedule calls" tab.

As we are looking for the number of days, the plan is not completed.

Can we get same data in any other list reports?

✍ ANSWER

Assuming you mean the date difference between planned and actual (confirmation date), this date can be found in tables MHIS and respectively.

☞ QUESTION 17

Issue Stock to PM Order

What is the best process to issue stock to an order?

For example if an order needs the stock not to be detailed within the original order, how does the store clerk add this additional stock to the order?

Obviously, it needs accounting for and has an impact on MRP. I assume there is a quicker and easier way of adding it without the store clerk going to change the order, adding the stock, then going to MIGO and doing an issue from reservation etc.

Is there a way to configure this to be more efficient?

✍ ANSWER

Check if it gives the hint of issuing the material which is not reserved in the work order.

For a more detailed procedure, please refer from:

http://help.sap.com/saphelp_47x200/helpdata/en/b0/df293581dc1f79e10000009b38f889/frameset.htm

☞ QUESTION 18

Warranty of spares

An urgent requirement from our clients is the capture of the warranty of spare parts. I know the warranty of equipment, function, and location. However, I am not up to date on how to check the warranty of material component when we create the order & assign the component to the orders which are under warranty. If there are any user exits available to check the warranty at the time of release or save and check the condition of component based on the characteristics value defined in the material master data classification. This will ensure that when the component is under warranty, the users do not save or release the order & give an error message to check the material under warranty.

I have created one material with a classification & assigned characteristics like a warranty counter or warranty period that defines the value in this classification. From here, the user can create the order for any equipment & assigned this material which act as a spare to order for repair (in case it needs one). When the user saves this order system to check the characteristics warranty period & counter for that material which are allocated in the component tab, the characteristics value exit for any material system will then throw a warning message that this material is under warranty. The user has to check the validity of warranty for that material manually.

The only thing missing from the configuration is the knowledge or know how on how to capture the warranty of spare parts. Where can I get this information and how do I capture the warranty of spare parts?

✍ ANSWER

This is regulation warranty for materials.

Follow the steps for compliance with regulation:

1) Go to the transaction BGM1;

2) Create master warranty screen will appear. From there, enter all the mandatory data;

3) Go to class, it will ask for class assignment, but don't assign any class there;

4) Now what you have to do is use transaction CL02 for creating class there in the basic data it will ask for validity. Enter from date and to date as warranty dates and save the class;

5) Assign the class to the meter warranty you created and save it.

This will work out and solve your problem even though it seems to be a crude method.

If the purpose of this is to serve only as an information message, then you could probably utilize user-exit CNEX0026 (general inspection of material).

You can view this user-exit via TCode SMOD.

☞ QUESTION 19

Message while completing RMA order

1. When we are technically completing the service order for RMA processing (SM03 in standard SAP), you get a message about the status of the repair materials. I understand that the 'free to be delivered' quantity is picked up from unrestricted sales order stock and 'blocked' quantity is picked up from the blocked sales order stock.

But how is the scrap quantity is picked up?

2. Is possible to issue the service material to the order and post back the repaired material into stock?

✍ ANSWER

The process I follow for the scrap in RMA is as follows:

1. Go to va02;
2. Select the line item;
3. Click repairs and mark scrap; The system will then give you a message saying "manual inventory is posting";
4. Does TECo. System will give you a message: "Free-to-delivery is 0 and scrapped is 1".

Use 551 mvt Type.

☞ QUESTION 20

Default equipment category

There is a requirement to default equipment category 'M' for certain users and 'P' for some other. In configuration, default equipment category is maintained as M.

Is there any way to assign 'P' to certain users?

✍ ANSWER

You could set the User's Parameter ID (PID) for this.

Set PID = EQT for Equip Category, Value = P.

☞ QUESTION 21

Access Control in Equipment Master

Equipment master consists of several tabs. It is possible to restrict access to some tabs when visited in change mode.

The client wants some tabs to appear in a display mode and some in change mode when equipment is visited through IE02.

How do I enforce this?

✍ ANSWER

Try Transaction and Screen Variants.

The T-CODE is SHD0.

☞ Question 22

Contract with several different billing value line items

We have service contracts with customers wherein we would like to bill them for the actual work done monthly instead of a fixed value (as determined by the monthly plan). We are certain to use contracts or else I could have used time and material to bill them.

Is there a way to force the contract to bill a certain value monthly based on the actual costs collected on the service orders for that month?

✍ Answer

Try settling all service order costs to the contract. After which, perform RRB on the contract itself (no billing plan required).

☞ QUESTION 23

Equipment & Functional Local Class

I would like to create one class for both function, location and equipment and then call it maintenance objects. I do know that you can allow multiple objects in the class type.

How do I set this up?

✍ ANSWER

You check in the IMG under Cross-Application Components->Classification.

☞ QUESTION 24

Equipment Classification

I have a Client that wants to have an equipment class automatically default to the equipment master during the create stage. The client also requires that when the equipment is either in display or change to display an information warning message prompting the user to review the classification and its associated characteristics.

I have checked the configuration for Classification and PM and haven't found anything that would satisfy the client's requirements. This appears be a custom change to the code.

How do I fulfill all the clients' requirements?

✍ ANSWER

You could create equipment with reference to another (say dummy master equipment).

Then utilize user-exit IEQM0003 (Additional checks before equipment update) to pop-up your warning message.

You could further investigate the following:

Use IEQM0003 to kick-off a batch program or workflow to re-enter the equipment (after initial save) and add data.

Create new event/method for business object EQUI (TCode SWO1).

☞ Question 25

Measuring Point

Can I maintain two different units in a measuring point?

For example:

I entered all readings in Amperes. Is it possible to maintain readings in Volts at the same time? If so, how do I go about this?

✍ Answer

You can have as many measurement points as you need.

You will need to create another measurement type (characteristic) to accommodate the other unit of measure.

Create a new measurement point with a new unit of measure and then link the new point with the old one using transmission of measurement reading. This will resolve your problem.

☞ QUESTION 26

Multiple counter plan with different cycle sets

The scenario is as follows:

If an equipment has following maintenance cycles:

1000 hrs or 250 liters
5000 hrs or 500 liters
10000 hrs or 1000 liters

The problem is that the maintenance steps are different for each of these cycle sets. In this scenario I am facing two problems:

The first is how to make a single maintenance plan which cover different cycle sets with different maintenance steps (task list).

The second is how do I create three separate cycle sets and use them in three different maintenance plans? Afterwards, how do I avoid scheduling of 1000 hrs or 250 liters once I schedule 5000 hrs or 500 liters?

✍ ANSWER

Enable the enhancement for the multiple counters in SPRO.

The path is PM&CS-->Maintenance Plans, Work centers, Task list, and PRTs-->Maintenance Plans-->Configure Special functions for maintenance planning.

Then, go through the documentation provided in the IMG before enabling this, as this setting will become irrevocable.

☞ QUESTION 27

Canceling refurbishment after costs are incurred

We utilize the Refurbishment process to refurbish our repairable spares. Our process is:

1) Create refurbishment order to repair a spare currently in inventory under the “damaged” valuation area. Target delivery is to the “repaired” valuation area.

2) Issue repairable spare from stock (valuation area “damaged”) to refurbishment order.

3) Begin in-depth inspection, proceed with repair.

4) Deliver repaired spare back to inventory (valuation area “repaired”).

5) TECO order.

In some cases, we may determine at step 3 that the spare is beyond repair. At this point the spare needs to be returned to inventory in the valuation area “damaged”, and subsequently scrapped.

We have been unable to find the functionality to allow us to return the spare to the “damaged” valuation area. It is not possible to change the target valuation area in the work order.

Has anyone developed a process to back out of refurbishment?

✍ ANSWER

Return the unit back to the repaired valuation area.

Then perform a stock-to-stock transfer from repaired to damaged.

Return the damaged item on the same order as damaged with a 262 (qty -1 on order).

Do transaction MB31 for zero qty and flag final delivery so that the work order can get status DLV.

If there are costs on the work order (i.e. cost of inspection) it is seen as an expense and settled to a CC.

☞ QUESTION 28

The combination of organizational data is not correct

I am working with CS. When using IW51 to create a notification for a customer I get the following information message:

"The combination of organizational data is not correct".

The message number is: QM 054

No more information is given. My parameters in my own data are the same as other users and they do not experience any problems with IW51.

The customer belongs to sales area 7000, dist. channel 10 and division 10. But I never get that far that I can choose a customer. I just get an initial screen, while others go directly into the notification.

Why is this happening and how do I resolve this?

✍ ANSWER

I'm assuming you have entered equipment in the notification.

If so, ensure that the sale organization of the customer is the same as the sales organization in the equipment master.

Verify if the customer belong to a sales area (sales order, dist channel, division).

Check this via TCode XD03.

☞ Question 29

Creating a subordinate Functional Location using BAPI

I'm trying to use BAPI_FUNCLOC_CREATE to create a subordinate Functional Location (ex., 1033-ADMI with superior functional location 1033 already established).

This BAPI ends with a blank/zero Return value but no updating is performed.

How do I fix this problem?

✍ Answer

You need to perform a "commit" function after the BAPI finishes.

☞ QUESTION 30

Master data changes in FL /EQUI

I have several related questions about the subject matter:

1. We are changing "Location" information in master data of FL and Equi. We want same changes reflected in the old notification and in the order of change objects.

The order table by direct way IAOL is FL/EQu table.

How can we accomplish this? How do I update notification?

2. What will be the fate of the PMIS info structures data (S061 etc), if I update the database table ILOA directly?

3. I also want to change the notification/order location data which is coming from ILOA table (which can be change in FL/EQ directly). When I am changing location data in FL, it's reflected in ILOA table but by close order/ notification, it's not showing updated location.

✍ ANSWER

Solutions are presented in the same number they were posed:

1. The only nice way is through the cancellation of business completion and TECO. Change the location, and then TECO, and business completion again.

This can be done with a CATT. A disadvantage could be

that the reference dates has the work order or notification change.

The quick and dirty solution is a direct update in table ILOA.

Another way is to talk to your ABAP team about “direct database updates” on table ILOA.

2. That will depend on the extent of PMIS usage. If you don’t use PMIS then it won’t matter.

3. When you create an Order/Notification, the location data is automatically copied (once only) from the FLoc/Equi. This copy function does NOT occur automatically again.

The following are now possible:

If no changes are made to the Equip/Floc/Order/Notif, then the data remains consistent.

You can change the data in the Floc/Equip. but the Order/Notif is not automatically updated with these changes.

You can change the data in the Order/Notif but the Floc/Equip is not automatically updated with these changes.

If you perform a right-click in the Order/Notif, there is a function Update reference object data which will re-copy the location data from the FLoc/Equip.

☞ Question 31

Automatic warranty dates update during equipment creation

I want to update warranty dates while creating the serial number and equipment during transaction outbound delivery. Can you please tell me the user exit for these?

✍ Answer

Investigate user-exit IQSM0007 (Serial numbers, user exit for goods movements).

☞ QUESTION 32

Revenue posting allowed for old orders

Concerning the indicator "Revenue posting allowed": we have set the indicator in the order type. It is copied from the order type when you create new orders.
But the orders that already exist are not changed when we set this indicator at a later date in the order type.

We have old orders and we need to use DP90 for these orders.

Is it possible to change this rule?

✍ ANSWER

The simple solution is to close the old orders, and re-create new ones.

☞ QUESTION 33

Need a field to store warranty against a sales order item

I am trying to change the way we calculate customer warranties.

Currently we use BGM2 to maintain materials that have warranty (our standard is 12 months). Then in a user exit in the outbound delivery screen we determine if a material has a master warranty and update the equipment records with the warranty begin date and the master warranty code.

However we also offer customers extended warranty on an order by order basis so I need to store any non-standard warranties against a sales order line, I will then check this before updating the equipment record, in the case of a non-standard warranty I will update the warranty begin and end dates. Currently, we are handling this by putting the extended warranty in sales texts and changing the equipment record manually.

Is there a good field to use for this? Are there any alternative solutions?

Just to make things slightly more complex whatever field I end up using will need to be able to be copied from contract to quote to sales order.

✍ ANSWER

I can think of two ways for this in the sales order:

1. Configurable materials i.e. using VC (usually not practical)

2. Create some new fields on the additional data tabs (header and item level)

Use the additional data tabs to do this and then used a batch program run overnight to work out what equipment records to update if the update is not needed immediately.

You don't need to use a user exit but SD is very good for user modifications. There are plenty of user exits and the documentation is very good too (unusual for SAP). In transaction SPRO, Sales and distribution->User Exits, there are user exits at all stages of the process. Click on the IMG activity document and the help will tell you the user exits and the program names.

☞ Question 34

Data origin change for address for EQUIPMENT/FL

We have very big hierarchies for Functional location/ equipment where address is inherited by FL/EQ lower down in hierarchy. Due to business reasons we want to maintain different addresses for FL/EQ (after three years of SAP!).

Following these moves, we have some questions:

Is there any risk (other than the data transfer flow for address) in doing this?

Are there any standard transaction/functions to carry this out en masse?

Is it ok to do this (inherited to individual) using SCAT script or IBIP/LSMW?

Are there any other problems that maybe caused by this?

How do we do "direct database update for the origin indicator (superior or individually maintained"?

✍ Answer

I don't see a major problem in theory.

In practice it may be a little tricky since you need to determine the correct address for each FLoc/Equip.

We did something similar a number of years back via ABAP program and it worked OK. From memory we did it via direct database update for the origin indicator (superior or individually maintained), then a function module to add the addresses to the technical object.

For the rest of your concerns, talk and coordinate with your ABAP team. They will know how to handle those.

With regards the last question, the fields are located in table ILOA, or EQUZ.

☞ QUESTION 35

Superior order and sub order

I want to use the sub-orders. However, I have a few doubts and would like to clarify some issues before I begin:

1) After the settlement of Sub order to Superior order, will I see the actual cost of Sub order in main work order?

2) Where can we find the list of sub order for one Superior order with all values and order numbers?

✍ ANSWER

Yes, there is a specific cost report in the order (Extras->Suborders->Cost overview).

The TCode IW38 uses the Leading order and the Superior order fields.

☞ Question 36

Structural display

I have the equipment and sub equipment.
My equipment is installed in functional location and the sub-equipment installed in equipment.

When I go to t.code IH01 I am not able to see the sub-equipment in that structural display.

What is the transaction to view all f/l, equipment and sub-equipment?

I have checked all boxes (Location hierarchy, Equipment Installed, Equipment Hierarchy, Expand Assembly, and Valid date is current date.). However, it is still showing F/L only.

I am using 4.7 version.

✍ Answer

Go into the FLoc (IL02) and display the structure list (button at top of the screen). Check if your equipment hierarchy is displayed.

If not, go to the equipment and check the details on the Structure tab. Also display the structure list.

If both of the above don't work, then it would appear to be a bug - check OSS using IH01 as search criteria.

☞ QUESTION 37

IP19 scheduling overview (Gantt chart)

I want to save the scheduling overview Gantt chart in excel format.

How can this be accomplished?

✍ ANSWER

The answer is to copy IP19 to your own program and add the required functionality.

This is a specialized area in which you need to know SAP's own programming language (called ABAP).

You should have a Development/Basis team somewhere within your project/company - ask them for a more detailed process.

☞ **QUESTION 38**

Message C7 057 No valid capacity for finite scheduling

The following message was received when trying to confirm an order:

"Work center has finite scheduling ticked".

The same Work center could confirm other orders. This is the first confirmation for the work center in question. Meanwhile, other confirmation exists for other work centers.

✍ **ANSWER**

Check to see if you have confirmed too much time for the same date with this work center.

If you are interested in finite capacity check, you can visit the site: http://digilander.libero.it/vietrim/index.html

There are some examples that show how a custom finite capacity check with sap screen examples works.

☞ QUESTION 39

Equipment installation at F/L

What is the purpose of "Position" field for equipment installation at functional location?

Can I give serial numbers like 1, 2, 3 ... for that or any other exact specification?

✍ ANSWER

On the definition of 'Position', 'Position' is when you install any equipment to give the analysis you need regarding a particular field. It is not mandatory but it all depends on your company structure or how you define the function location.

By default, the SAP system sort in the hierarchy, the pieces of equipment by alphanumerical order. If you use the position field, your equipment will be sorted by the value of this field.

An example may be a pump-bay with four pumps:

The pump-bay may be represented in SAP as a single Functional Location. The four pumps would then be four Equipment masters.

The positions of the pumps (equipment) in the pump-bay (Field Location) could be 1, 2, 3 and 4.

☞ QUESTION 40

Availability Control for Cost Center

The requirement is that the client wants to control the Budget at Cost Center level.

Budget is maintained for Cost Centers using the TCode KPZ2 for the Fiscal year month wise. At the time of posting Goods Issue or Time Confirmation or Service Entry Sheet for the Maintenance Order, if the amount exceeds the Budget, the system should give message.

For Order and Project, availability control is there by default in SAP.

Could you please give some input on budget control at Cost Centers?

✍ ANSWER

I think the control can be established when requesting for the resources.

Example: raising a PR, after the release of a PR, and goods procured.

The scenario is for Expenses Budget for the Cost Center.

The Engineering Department gives Expenses Budget (Includes Manpower cost, Spares, External Services) for the fiscal year with a monthly break up.

Using the TCode KPZ2, the Budget values will be maintained.

Let us take an example Budget for January 2006 for the Cost Center Engineering Department is $500,000. At the time of posting transactions like Goods Issue, Service Entry Sheet or Time Confirmation, if the total expenses for the month of January exceeds the Budget value $500,000, the system should give the message.

☞ QUESTION 41

Billing Plan

When creating the billing document from the repair request the billing date is taking the repair request create date. How do I appoint the billing date as the current date?

✍ ANSWER

Have a look in the header of the 'repair order'. There, you should find the billing date.

Typically, this is used by the billing due list (TCode VF04) to determine when to invoice the customer.

☞ QUESTION 42

Multiple counter plans with hierarchy

We're currently running strategy-based PM plans that contain different visits. Example: Every 2000 machine hours we do a small visit, every 4000 machine hours a larger visit and so on. We have set this up with hierarchies, meaning that at e.g. 4000 machine hours, only the large visit takes place, and the small visit is suppressed.

This works fine, but we want to extend this to both counter and time based. Example: a large visit every 4000 machine hours, or every year, whichever is reached first. From what I've seen, we cannot use priorities in multiple counter plans. Is this correct?

There was an enhancement with 4.7 - you're supposed to be able to use 2 cycle sets in the plan. I tested it using my first cycle set of every 5,000 miles or 6 months (whichever came first) and my second cycle set at every 40,000 miles or 24 months (whichever came first). The first cycle set was triggering correctly, however the second cycle set doesn't trigger correctly based on the counter. Time wise it was working. I did an OSS note but got no where. They were basically telling me it worked just fine based on time.

How do I use the enhancement and get the second cycle to trigger correctly based on a counter?

✍ ANSWER

You can't use the package and hierarchy concept in multi-counter plans. But I remember vaguely that something was foreseen in 4.7 extension set 200.

There are some alternative avenues you might want to pursue:

Investigate user-exit IPRM0002 (Determine planned date info for maintenance plan).

Alternatively, you could stick with your strategy-based maintenance plans and develop an ABAP program to give you the required functionality.

It could work something like this:

1. Run batch program before your IP30 run (date monitoring program);
2. Program determines if the time-period is exceeded (e.g. 1 year);
3. If exceeded, manually call the next maintenance visit;
4. Run IP30 as usual;

If you decide to go down this route, make sure you test it thoroughly.

☞ QUESTION 43

Requirement date for components

Can anyone tell me if it's possible to have different requirements dates for materials on the component list of a work order.

We have a number of components that are required on different days.

I tried using the off-set, but with no luck.

It appears that the requirement date is the same as the basic start date; can this be changed for each component?

✍ ANSWER

You can check the 'scheduling parameters' in customizing. You need an option with 'operation dates' in stead of 'order dates'.

The standard setting for PM and CS orders is forward scheduling.

The planned-dates for components therefore take the start-date of the operation (not order header) as the starting point for the calculation. Days are added/subtracted from various dates in the order and material master to determine the estimated delivery dates.

This is performed for each individual material/component.

Take note that each component can have a different offset.

☞ QUESTION 44

Refurbishment of parts

Here is the scenario with my client:

1) My client buys bulk scrap by weight (Lbs/Kgs).He does not know at the time of receipt what parts come with the scrap.

2) When there is a requirement for refurbishing the parts they create a Work order and issue the scrap in weight (e.g. 100 lbs of some 1000lbs of scrap in inventory) to the Work Order. Add labor and other parts and make a refurbished part. Their labor codes are service materials of type DIEN. My client also uses split valuation. My client also sends out parts for third party refurbishment if they can not be done in-house.

3) My client also wants to capture the actual cost of refurbishing each part (Cost of labor and materials) since these will be sold at actual cost of Refurbishment + Margin. Note that this may be different for two similar parts so I can not settle this to Material. The client uses valuation at std cost.(No MAP)

I need help on whether I need to use the PM refurbishment order or do I use the service order. What is the repair order scenario for this? Can you explain the steps in this process?

How do I capture the actual refurbishment costs on the sales order?

✍ Answer

I think you will need to use the repair order option. This will allow you to return the item(s) into stock (maybe special Stock Location), and then decide if a service order is required.

However, you will not be able to use DIEN materials in the service order for labor costs/codes.

☞ QUESTION 45

Authorization and order type

We must create an activity group which allows users to create, change and display certain order types. Also we must add authorization for another order type for these users, but they should only be able to display these orders. Our release is 46B. We don't have user-exit IWO10033.

✍ ANSWER

This can be done in 4.6 with PFCG. But if you're in 46B, the only thing I can think of is putting some validation in the customer exit of the work order and save. I agree it's a bit late in the process, but it's better than nothing.

☞ QUESTION 46

Maintenance Plan

We have created one Plan area wise / Section wise Machineries, at header level given one Equipment & others attached in the Object list.

The system is generating order for header Equipment & history also on the same list.

Is it possible we can see or maintain history for all equipment which are attached in the object list?

Can the system generate a different order for each of the equipment?

Is there any other solution to maintain the history for all these equipment by a single Plan?

✍ ANSWER

The system will create a call-object (order, notification, etc) for each maintenance item in the maintenance plan. It does not create a call-object for items in the object list.

Therefore, to answer your question, create additional maintenance items in the maintenance plan and link each to equipment.

☞ Question 47

Document flow in the Maintenance order

I combine several notifications to one Maintenance order using tcode 'IW32', and when I display document flow in the Maintenance order, I find that it only can show one pm notification, and it can't display other notifications.

Can anyone tell me how to display the other notifications in the document flow of the Maintenance order?

✍ Answer

The other notifications can be found on the 'object list' tab.

Once in IW32, just click on the tab page with the label 'objects'.

☞ QUESTION 48

Measuring Points

We have created a Measuring Point for the Measurement of the Vibration of Machine & the given Target Value of Vibration. Is it possible if the vibration level is more than the targeted value and then automatically "Notification" will be generated by the system?

✍ ANSWER

Search for the 'condition based maintenance' on data within the system. It will provide you the necessary processes involved and verification of data you have queried.

☞ QUESTION 49

Released Schedule

Does anyone know how I can be able to identify when a work order is released? I only found the date when the order was released, but I can't find anything on what time of the day the order was released.

What table can this be checked with?

Where in the transaction can this be located?

Is there any function or further steps with which this can be identified (function module, bapi, etc)?

✍ ANSWER

Have a look in the action or changes log within the order.

Go to the status screen and select the REL status. Use the menu path Extras >Change documents > For status. This will show date, time, and user.

☞ QUESTION 50

Warranty Costs

There is one query for warranty costs. What we are doing is using the accounting indicator to show goods that are under warranty. When we do the billing it takes zero value as accounting indicator has -100% in condition records.

Now after billing the value categories in the service order is showing the warranty costs as the negative of revenue. Is it correct or accurate?

I will explain with an example:

The cost of a good is Rs 20(ek01) but the sales price is Rs 100 (PR00). When it is under warranty it is showing -100 as the warranty costs instead of 20 because we have assigned the sales price to KBM1 condition type(-100%) to cancel it. Is it the right way?

It is showing warranty costs as Rs 100 in the value category. How can I show the actual costs as warranty costs?

How can I show the cost in the warranty value category?

Right now my warranty costs are showing Rs 100. Should it show Rs 100 or Rs 10 as warranty costs?

✍ ANSWER

This is the standard way to use the accounting indicator: that the costs will not change.

An alternative is to settle the costs from the service order to a special account for warranty.

Change your pricing procedure to ignore EK01.

This could be achieved in many ways e.g. make the line statistical only, use ABAP, etc.

Talk to your local SD team, they should be able to advise.

EK01 represents the cost of the item to your company.

PR00 represents the sales price (revenue) to the customer.

In your case the revenue is zero (PR00) but it still cost your company money to perform the service (EK01).

Here is an example of the standard pricing procedure PSER02:

EK01: 100EUR
PR00: 500EUR
Total: 500EUR

Now add 100% discount
EK01: 100EUR
PR00: 500EUR
KBM1: -100%
Total: 100EUR

If you want the total to be zero, then you will need to change your pricing procedure.

☞ QUESTION 51

Storage Location in PM

We have a problem here. Our design is, the delivery address in the Purchase Order is deriving from the Storage location. So, when creating the request from work order, we enter the material master (if it is stock item) as well as the storage location, vendor details, etc, under the Component tab. Then, the storage location will be defaulted into PR, then PO. Hence, the delivery address is there.

But in service, I can't enter any Storage Location. Is there a solution for this?

If I create the service in PM (via IW31), is there a way for me to enter the Storage Location?

✍ ANSWER

Storage locations are only used when issuing/receiving stock into the warehouse.

I think the delivery address can only be entered for non-stock materials. This makes sense since you are delivering a physical object to a particular location.

Services are not stock/non-stock items and I suspect you cannot enter a SLoc or delivery address.

You could try user-exits/batch program which allocates the address dependent upon some information from the order.

Have a look at the services user-exits via TCode SMOD and search criteria SRV*.

☞ QUESTION 52

Determine task processor automatically at save

Is it possible to determine header tasks automatically at Save without selecting the Save + Determine tasks button? The users only want to click the Save button and trigger the Save + Determine tasks. How do I program this?

✍ ANSWER

It is possible if there is an IMG setting for automatic task determination on save.

Another to do this via one of the following user-exits:

QQMA0014: Checks before saving a notification;

ICSV0002: Automatic task determination for service notifications;

☞ QUESTION 53

Inspection points in the task list

There is an inspection point facility in the task list where we can put qualitative and quantitative values for inspection. Once we call the task list in the work order the operation details comes in the work order but the details of inspection points are not displayed in the work order neither I find any facility to view the inspection points details. I think we need to use inspection points for inspection type of work order.

In my case inspection lot is not created automatically, rather, it has to be created manually. My scenario is that during schedule inspection inspectors are going to inspect a particular area in which they have to check many inspection points both quantitative and qualitative. In this case we are creating a task list in which we define all the inspection points with target values. Once we call the task list in the maintenance plan and run it, work order is created but the information of inspection point is not indicated in the work order and neither will the inspection lot be created.

I am using inspection point 300 for equipment and maintaining inspection points in the task list. However, once I carry out scheduling, run work order is created but no inspection lot is created. How do I create an inspection lot automatically from the scheduling run?

✍ ANSWER

When you are creating the MIC by QS21, at that time u have to define the particular characteristics as Qualitative or quantitative.

If you want to see the inspection characteristics in work order you have to check the inspection lot. There you will get all the information about characteristics and range that you defined in the task list.

I am not 100% sure, but the inspection point concept is extensively used in production processes and specifically in the repetitive manufacturing. In the case of PM, by selecting equipment as the inspection point (300) you can continue to put the equipment number and do result in recording.

In the IMG 'Assign Inspection Types to Maintenance/Service Order Types', check whether the Inspection type 14 is set for your plant and order type (which you are using in your 'inspection' plans).

Just check you inspection plan status, once it is released.

The inspection lot should generate when the maintenance order is released.

☞ QUESTION 54

TECO Order

I have some issues pertaining to Work order.

The users technically complete the work orders and settle it. However, they come back after a few days and cancel the technical completion and post against the work order. This must be a posting a problem as it is not posting to the correct cost center.

I have two questions about this:

1. Is there a setting such that once an Order is TECO, work completion cannot be cancelled?

2. How can I stop a user from posting anything in TECO Orders?

✍ ANSWER

Answers are given in the order they were asked:

1. Authorization object I_VORG_ORD is checked through:

AUTHORITY-CHECK OBJECT 'I_VORG_ORD'
ID 'BETRVORG' FIELD BETRVORG
ID 'AUFART' FIELD AUART.

Where BETRVORG equals 'BUTA';

But, also in TECO, people can consume (unplanned) materials or confirm work hours; you might want to double check if blocking the un-TECO would resolve your problem.

There is an alternative solution:

Utilize a user-exit to pop-up a warning/error message when creating a confirmation document.

Have a look at TCode SMOD with a search criteria CONFPM*;

It's just an alternative option to investigate. The first solution was better but it wouldn't work for goods movements via IW41, but not for POs, SES, etc.

User-statuses could also cause problems e.g.
- PR created in REL status
- PO created in REL status
- Order TECO'ed and user-status blocks goods movements;
- Now try to GR the PO - you will now get a status error.

At some level you need to control processes via training/ education etc.

2. You can do this by using a user profile, in which a status is activated automatically by the TECO business process.

To this user status, you can block 'actual postings';

☞ QUESTION 55

Table for Activity Planned Costs

Can someone tell me the tables in CO for actual costs by activity type?

✍ ANSWER

You can try COEP, COSP, COSS, COST, and BSEG.

☞ Question 56

How to add new TCode to table T365

I want to add a new Z transaction that will be used only for the creation of a special notification type. The problem is, I can not configure a default value for a transaction that does not exist on table T365.

The version we use is 4.6C

I tried via SM30 but it is a repair function.

How can I maintain the table?

✍ Answer

You can try TCode SM30 or SE11 instead.

Try entering T365 in SM30 and then pressing the customizing button (or similar).

This should bring up a list of IMG elements where T365 can be configured.

Go to SE16> give table name T365>there is a create button, Put your Tcode & program name;

☞ QUESTION 57

Change estimated costs on a CS order

I have read from previous posts that it is not possible in standard SAP to change the estimated costs for released service orders.

Has there been a system modification implemented to change this and make it possible? What do you have to change to enable the user exit?

✍ ANSWER

You cannot change the estimated costs once the order is released.

But I believe that it is possible via a "direct database update". Coordinate the task with your ABAP team as they are in a position to help.

☞ QUESTION 58

Linking maintenance plan category to number range

I have created an external number range for maintenance plans, and a maintenance plan category for maintenance orders. In SPRO I can add an external range number, but when I tried to save, the value isn't saved.

Is there another way of linking these two functions?

✍ ANSWER

If there have been any warning or error messages displayed, please include message number e.g. AB 055.

In IP20, select the relevant unassigned MPC (little button), select the relevant number range and press the big button to assign.

☞ QUESTION 59

Table and field for notification status

Which are the exact SAP table and field for SAP PM Notification status?

✍ ANSWER

The easiest way is to use function module STATUS_TEXT_EDIT.

You can find the PM/CS tables here.

☞ QUESTION 60

Notification mail

I have one issue with my client. The Production people will create the Notification. With reference to that Notification Maintenance people will create the Maintenance order.

My requirement is:

When ever they create Notification the Maintenance people should receive an automatically generated email.

1) Is it possible to generate email to a particular user in SAP?

2) Is it possible to generate email to a particular user in Outlook express?

✍ ANSWER

There are several options for emailing in SAP. Here are some:

1. Use standard Workflow functions to send email to SAP Inbox.

2. Synchronize your SAP inbox with Outlook/Lotus Notes etc.

3. Use custom developments to send emails (user-exits, BADIs, etc).

☞ QUESTION 61

DIP Profile

I have just set-up a repair order in which this repair order creates a service order to record repair activities. The RRB profile is located on the repair order. When the goods movement is done on a service order, it will basically capture the actual cost.

Now when it comes to billing, I will need to execute dp90 on the repair order. Unfortunately the systems give me an error message:

'No expenditure item found'.

However, there are expenditure items found on the service order.

How can this be resolved?

✍ ANSWER

Do the following to correct the situation:

Make sure that you run DP90 with the sales order number and not the service order. Go back to the service order and check if there are actual costs involved.

Check your DIP Profile; specifically the sources section to ensure that you are not filtering out any dynamic items.

Check the planned/actual report (button) in the Cost tab; check that a quantity is displayed.

☞ **QUESTION 62**

Automatic release of PM order creating from notification

Can we do the automatic release of the maintenance order when we create the order from maintenance notification? I had set the automatic relay in customizing for the order.

But when I create the order from notification, the system does not set the status relay for the maintenance order. How can I fix this?

✍ **ANSWER**

You can read the help-text in the IMG for that field. It explains in detail the processes for which this functionality applies.

Initially, you can investigate user-exit IWO10009 (at save).

Then, you should still be able to utilize IWO10009 to check if a notification has been assigned (possibly via the program stack).

You should also get your ABAP team to get involved and check the problem.

☞ QUESTION 63

Tables storing the priorities, notification types

I need for the tables to be able to provide the priority configuration. A table that store notification types and a table that stores the work order types.

Where do I find the configuration function for this?

✍ ANSWER

Check in the PM/CS links. There you'll find an entry to PM tables.

☞ QUESTION 64

Business Area

Does anyone know how a Business Area defaults into the Add Data Tab page on a Work Order (even though the Business Area field is hidden in configuration)?

✍ ANSWER

Go to iw32> Extras-->Settings -->Default values -in General; There you can set the business area, planning plant, and profit center etc.

☞ Question 65

PP-PM integration

We have a requirement at our client place.

At the time of production confirmation using transaction code C011, the system has to cumulate the confirmed production quantities. When it reaches a certain quantity (Ex: 100 tons), the system should generate the maintenance order in Plant maintenance.

Is there any possibility for configuration in SAP for the above-mentioned query?

What is the appropriate formula or configuration step?

Should we create the equipment as PRT equipment (Equipment category as PRT)?

✍ Answer

There is an integration of PP-PM in case of PRTs, wherein you can create measuring documents for usage of PRT when you do confirmation using CO11. This will in turn create the maintenance order as PRT.

You can use the equipment for which you need to create the maintenance order as PRT in the routing of PP and for the PRT you have to put in the formula for calculating its usage.

When you do the confirmation for the produced material the formula will update the usage of PRT which will in turn create a measuring document.

Try to do the above.

Or you can try creating that equipment as PRT. The formulas are on the same line as the formulae that you create for work centre.

☞ QUESTION 66

Priority types in order

I have configured the priority types for order PM and was able to assign on each order types. But the priority types are not working (activated). However, in notifications, the priority types are working correctly.

How do I correct this error and provide some consistency on the processes involved?

✍ ANSWER

If you get a warning or error message give the message number e.g. AB 055.

The work order priorities are not influencing the basic dates, unless you enter the priority on the very first screen.

There is however a customer exits available to implement the same behavior as in the notification.

Check the IW* customer exits to confirm functionality.

☞ QUESTION 67

Additional data in equipment master

I would like to activate the user fields in Equipment Master but unable to do it. I only managed to activate the additional data TAB. The new TAB is blank. Example: 'no field is displayed'.

How can I fulfill this requirement?

✍ ANSWER

You should considered classification.

Alternatively, investigate user-exit ITOB0001 (sub screen for technical. object master data) via TCode SMOD.

Or BADIs EQUI_SCR_* (via TCode SE18);

You may also try searching SAPFans using ITOB0001.

☞ QUESTION 68

Maintenance order not generating in counter based planning

I am facing a problem in the maintenance schedule plan.

1. Strategy plan

A maintenance plan is scheduled for every 100 hrs, where the maintenance order should generate for every 100 hrs. However, I am facing problem whenever the measuring document has completed more than 100 hrs. reading, because the maintenance order is not created. Below are the steps I have taken:

-Characteristic-Hours;
-Created measuring point with annual estimate 3650;
-Measuring document created for more than 100 hrs;
-Scheduling period is for 90 days;

2. Multiple counter plan with OR condition i.e. 300hr or 300km.

In multiple counter plans, I also did a schedule but when the measuring document created more than 300 km, I am not getting the maintenance order. Below should be the indicative factors:

- Characteristic—Hours;
- Created measuring point with annual estimate 3650;
- Measuring document created for 200 hrs;
- Characteristic—Kilo meters;
- Created measuring point with annual estimate 3650;
- Measuring document created for more than 300 km.;

I did all scheduling through IP10.

How do I correct the problem?

✍ ANSWER

You need to re-schedule the maintenance plan(s) after each measurement document is entered.

This is usually achieved via TCode IP30 which is set to run periodically (batch).

☞ Question 69

Batch job for Automatic settlement of Maintenance Orders

I have to schedule a Batch job on a daily basis for the settlement of Maintenance Orders.

I have chosen transaction KO8G and defined a variant inside it. The variant defined have selection parameters mentioned below - Controlling are/Company Code/Order type [Range]/All;

Status is checked like CRTD/REL/TECO/COMP.

However, the problem is in the transaction KO8G - there is only one entry field for settlement period. I can only give one period. For example, say (1). However, when the same job would run in the next period, say (2), how do I get this to change to (2)?

Furthermore, as I understand it, I have to mention a "Status Selection Profile" in the variant with "REL" or "TECO" in the customizing of Selection Profiles in order to further define that only Orders with these system statuses should be chosen.

Also, in the transaction there is a field called Settlement Period and fiscal Year. Do I have to change this field manually for each batch job? If so, this means that I can't run this on daily basis.

How do I schedule all of these as a background job?

✍ Answer

In the definition of the variant, you can specify fields from table TVARV. One of those is 'current period'. 'Current year' is also available.

Each time the program with the variant is run, the 'actual' values of TVARV are determined.

Of course, the value of 'current period' must be updated each month.

One comment though: It doesn't make sense to settle the CRTD orders.

There is also no need for CLSD or a status selection profile.

☞ QUESTION 70

Goods Issues to Service Orders across Company Codes

I have segregated several questions according to the relevance of their topics:

Question A:

Is it possible to issue stock direct to a Service Order within a different company code?

What specifics would need to be set to ensure that the finances post correctly?

Are there any specific business considerations that need to be taken into account for this process to work?

Question B:

I am assuming that the next stage would be for CC2 to create a billing document and CC1 to enter the invoice for payment on to the system?

Can all of this be avoided to bring the whole process into some back ground financial transactions to get the costs straight onto the Service Order?

Where can I get a copy of the MB1A 261 movement issues CC2 stock to the CC1 Service Order?

✍ ANSWER

Answers were given as they were grouped:

Answer A: Yes it is possible.

You need to talk to your MM team about this.

If you are interested in implementing it yourself, the basic process is as follows:

1. Create PM/CS order with non-stock materials (CC1)
2. Order creates a PR (CC1)
3. Create a PO from the PR and assign inter-company-vendor for CC2
4. Create Delivery document (CC2)
5. Goods issue from delivery document (CC2)
6. Goods receipt for PO (CC1)
7. Create billing document (type IV) from CC2 to CC1

Answer B:

Yes, there is an inter-company billing document (type IV) created from CC2 to CC1.

All processes can be amended accordingly as required.

☞ QUESTION 71

Table that contains both measuring point and equipment

Can you tell me which table contains both a measuring point and equipment number, and a measuring point and functional location?

The purpose in finding one is to find a corresponding equipment or function location for a given measuring point.

In EQUI (equipment master table) the values for the field IMRC_POINT is blank corresponding to equipment number which is having a measuring point.

Given the above data, how do I find this table?

✍ ANSWER

Try the following:

Equipment: EQUI-OBJNR->IMPTT-MPOBJ;

FLoc: IFLOT-OBJNR->IMPTT-MPOBJ;

☞ QUESTION 72

Report connects between maintenance plan and its task list

Is there a report that can show me a maintenance plan and all its task lists?

✍ ANSWER

You need a list-edit report for maintenance items. Look for IP18.

☞ Question 73

The Authorization Object WERKS in IA25 transaction

When deleting a Task List in IA25, only I_ROUT object is being checked for the Field ACTVT to be with values 24 & 41.

This means that the person from Plant 1 can delete Task Lists from Plant 2.

Therefore, the Authorization Object WERKS is not checked!

How do I correct this?

✍ Answer

See if there is an authorization object for IWERK (planning plant). From there, do the revisions as needed to comply with your requirement.

☞ Question 74

Creating Person responsible and Department responsible

How do I create a person responsible and department responsible which are related to NOTIFICATIONS T-CODE IW21?

✍ Answer

A Person responsible (employee no./personnel no.) and Department are to be created as HR master records.

☞ QUESTION 75

Costing variant for PM orders

I intend to use the standard Costing Variant for PM Orders.

What are the Standard costing variants used for PM Orders?

If I use the standard costing variant, is it necessary to assign a costing type and valuation variant to it?

✍ ANSWER

The standard planned/actual costing variants are both set to PM01.

Your FI/CO team may need to adjust the costing type and valuation variant etc.

Either way, coordinate with your FI/CO team about these settings.

☞ Question 76

Final configuration

What is the difference between Baseline configuration and Final configuration?

✍ Answer

It depends on the implementation methodology you are using (e.g. ASAP).

Typically speaking, baseline configuration is a basic set-up to demonstrate processes to the business.

The final configuration would then be the final design ready for go-live.

☞ QUESTION 77

PM02 work order

I am reviewing the requirements for PM reporting and one of the requests is to change the SAP system configuration to not allow manual PM02 type work orders through the following transactions: IH01, IW31, IW24, IW25, IW26 and ZIW26. An added requirement is to display a hard error if a client tries to create a PM02 work order through one of these transactions.

Can anyone please let me know how to approach and accomplish this requirement?

✍ ANSWER

You can try using Authorizations on the TCode and Order Type.

This is absolutely possible by restricting authorizations by PM order type.

Do it through the authorization objects: I_AUART and I_TCODE.

Lastly, check and coordinate with your authorization people.

☞ QUESTION 78

About the release of the Maintenance order

When I have already released one maintenance order and want to retract the order, how do I go about canceling the release?

✍ ANSWER

You cannot reverse the REL status back to CRTD status.

Standard status flow: CRTD->REL->TECO->CLSD;

However, you can cancel both the TECO and CLSD statuses.

You can also postpone an order through:

Go to "Order-->Functions-->Complete-->Cancel TECO or Cancel Business Completion;

☞ QUESTION 79

POPUP Screen

I have a requirement from the client to popup the history of the equipment at the time of creating service notification of the same equipment.

Is this possible? If so, how do I go about it?

✍ ANSWER

Yes, it is possible. Activate the object information & give the time for which you need the history pop ups.

There is also a user-exit to support the standard object information functionality (see ICSV0004: Check PM object and display object information).

☞ QUESTION 80

Settlement of Maintenance Order

If settlement will not run for Maintenance Orders, what is the repercussion?

How will this affect business?

✍ ANSWER

You may have several effects:

1. You may not be able to close the orders (CLSD);
2. You may not post the costs in the correct period;
3. In CS, contract profitability may be distorted;

☞ QUESTION 81

Auto creation of Equipment master from GI=>Asset

1. I would like to know whether there is a possibility to automatically create an equipment master from an asset created due to GI of material from inventory. If yes, how can this be accomplished?

I'm currently using serial with no functionality.

2. How can I create an asset master from equipment master automatically?

✍ ANSWER

Responses are given according to the number they were asked:

1. You cannot use a serial number and asset accounting together. But it is possible to create an equipment master automatically from an asset (or vice versa). Check the IMG nodes under Financial Accounting > Asset Accounting > Master Data > Automatic Creation of Equipment Master Records.

Have a quick look on OSS and perform the following:

-Goods issue creates serial number;
--Serial number creates equipment;
---Equipment creates asset master;

However I suspect the reverse is not possible (automatically).

2. Its set-up is somewhere in the Asset Accounting IMG.

Talk to your FI/CO team about this activity.

☞ Question 82

Exit to check and change data on save in Service order

1. I need to check and change some data while saving the service order (for example based on planner group we want to change the material supply plant in the components screen - IW31&IW32).

Are there any preferred exits for this?

2. I tried these 2 exits and I am able to validate & display a message but the client requirement is to change the data. Are there any BADI for this?

✍ Answer

Answers are given according to the number they were asked:

1. I don't think there is a user-exit to change the data on saving.

Instead, you could validate the data and issue a message by using one of the following user-exits:

IWO10009: Check for 'Save' Event;
PPCO0001: Application development: PP orders;

2. You can view BADIs via TCode SE18.

Try conducting a search using ALM* or IW*.

You can also check out Customer exit CNEX0027 (EXIT_SAPLCOMK_007) Customer Enhancement: Plant and Storage Location Determination.

The documentation states:

" You can use this customer exit to perform a plant or location determination for a component.

The system processes the function module when a bill of material or a task list is included, as well as when components are entered manually in the component list.

☞ QUESTION 83

Changing the Planning Plant in task list

If I want to change the Planning Plant for the task list, how should I proceed?

✍ ANSWER

It cannot be actually be changed, but you can modify a particular Equipment in IE02 -> in Organization -> Responsibility -> Planning Plant.

You can also change IP05 in the Planning Data.

☞ QUESTION 84

Number range for PM orders

I am facing a problem regarding the number range in PM orders in customizing.

I had given a common number range to all the PM orders that is 9000000 to 9999999. However, when we started to create PM01 it starts with 9000000 and goes up to 9000003 for the 4 orders. After this, we started to create PM02 and the systems start the number from 9000020. Hence, we lost the remaining number range from 9000004 to 9000019.

In current number range it is also showing 9000039. It is taking a batch of 20 for the orders.

Why is this happening?

How can I correct the situation?

✍ ANSWER

This sounds like a buffering problem.

You can try searching OSS. It could also be something to do with the application servers allocating a certain amount of numbers.

Ask and Coordinate with your Basis team.

An alternative approach would be:

During the configuration, define the number range like it is configured below - for example:

PM01 1xxxxxxx to 1xxxxxxx
PM02 2xxxxxxx to 3xxxxxxx
PM03 4xxxxxxx to 4xxxxxxx

Hence, it will show the different number for PM01 and then For PM02.

If you still get this skipping range problem for the same type, then you really have to inform your BASIS team.

Here's a 2nd alternative answer:

The 'skipping' of nos. is fairly common. Check out SAP note 62077 to understand the phenomenon, the solution (no buffering) & the problems if it is the buffering will be deactivated.

Interaction steps:

Separate the number ranges for each order type. It will reduce the buffering problems and give an immediate identifier of the order type i.e. PM01 = 6000000, PM02 = 7000000 etc.

Different number ranges can then be used in many of the list-edit reports such as IW38.

Remember that with number ranges, you do NOT to take up all the available number range (e.g. 0 to 9999999999999999). If you do, this will cause you problems in the future.

☞ QUESTION 85

Object information keys

I have assigned Object information keys (PM) to Maintenance order, but I find that when I create order in the object information section, the field of OrdsCrtd is not automatically updated

How can I fix this issue?

✍ ANSWER

You need to save the order(s) before they are even registered. This will fix your issue.

☞ Question 86

Postponement of Order

Can we postpone all planned orders for a specified period of time?

It means whenever the plant is under shutdown for 30 Days, major work in that duration will not be generated.

✍ Answer

You may use revisions for rescheduling the orders. I am not aware of any method to "stop" the planned orders getting generated.

Assuming that you are talking about orders generated from maintenance plans, here's what you can do to resolve the problem:

1. Skip the relevant calls via TCode IP10.

2. Alternatively investigate user-exit IPRM0002 (Determine planned date info for maintenance plan).

3. By ip02 you can lock the order and when you require the service again, you can unlock the same.

To unlock, do the following:

1. Go to IP02—> maintenance plan—> function—>active /inactive—>deactivate.

2. Check the schedule. You will find the schedule locked.

Hence you will not get any order for your specified time.

Until you un-lock the plan, IP30 will then try to create the back-logged orders.

Deactivating a maintenance plan is not the same as locking an order.

☞ QUESTION 87

Four doubts in CS

I have been assigned an additional responsibility of handling the CS module. Though I have undergone CS training at the SAP academy, I have some basic doubts and would be thankful if somebody can clarify them.

1. Construction type: How useful is this? Can I be given an example of this for better understanding?

2. A group of machines is delivered at the customers site (for each an equipment master is created). Now notifications will be raised on a single Equipment number.

   How can I see the defects in the notification reports by selecting only one equipment number? For this, do I have to use some other technical object for grouping them together?

3. Can I have an alphanumerical serial numbers which I will assign during the deliveries?

4. If the owners (customer) of the equipment changes how do I update the equipment master with this change?

✍ ANSWER

For the first question, you alone can determine this as you go along the new functions assigned to you.

Answer to 2nd:

First of all you cannot group the equipment and raise the

notification. Either you create a function location and install the relative equipment under that and create a notification against that function location. This will help you if done properly.

Answer to 3rd: You can configure this to happen.

Answer to 4th:

Your master data of equipment is to be maintained as per manufacturer name and not on customer name. Equipment is installed at function location and that will come under a maintenance plant and the company code. These are basic things and rules you have to comply with.

Also, if that customer is defined as in the above hierarchy, then you have to dismantle the equipment and transfer to the relevant particular company code.

There is an alternative solution:

1. For the construction type:

   This is used in two main ways; to assign a material BOM which you can explode in the order to obtain maintenance spares, and/or to denote the material required to replace the whole equipment.

   As a standard, you can only use the Material BOM (construction type) in PM/CS orders and NOT in sales orders.

2. Machine Groups: Use the list-edit reports.

   There is no such field as machine groups. Common methods are to be used in the customer (sold-to party) or functional location as grouping functions.

3. Investigate user-exit IQSM0001 (Automatic serial number assignment).

4. Customer Equipment:

   Change the equipment manually. Or like many customers do, write an ABAP program to update equipment after delivery to customer.

   Many clients prefer to use the Sold-to Party instead (customer).

☞ QUESTION 88

Equipment history update for Spare parts

I am not able to give the equipment no. in the spare part sales order. This would update the history of equipment and the client can track all the spare parts delivered or consumed for the equipment.

Is it possible to give the equipment no. in sales order similar to service and maintenance contract type?

Where can the equipment no. be given? Will this update the equipment master history automatically?

I had tried this option earlier, only that the client was not comfortable in executing one extra sales transaction. It looks like there is no other option but to convince them on this.

Is there any other solution to this problem?

✍ ANSWER

You have several options on how to approach this.

1. You can create a new sales document with type "contract".

2. You can also use serial numbers.

You can also raise an OSS Message to SAP asking them if its possible to create a sales order via VA01 and still have the technical object list.

☞ QUESTION 89

PM order with material cost

When I execute a PM work order with materials linked to it, I am not able to get the planned cost / actual values of the materials with the cost elements.

What is the appropriate setting that needs to be done in order to capture the material costs with cost elements?

✍ ANSWER

You can do the following:

1. Ensure your materials have a valuation class assigned.

2. Ensure your order has planned/actual costing variants assigned (last tab).

3. Ensure your value categories are correct.

4. Check the costs via the planned/actual report button on the Cost tab.

☞ QUESTION 90

Collective release

How can I release the collective Preventive maintenance orders?

✍ ANSWER

Try using TCode IW38 by entering your order type for ‘Preventive maintenance orders’.

Once in the list-display, select the relevant order and use menu-path:

Order->Release order.

Alternatively, set the Release immediately flag in the order type customizing (TCode OIOA).

☞ QUESTION 91

Flow path of maintenance order

What is the flow path of maintenance order?

I am not sure whether technical completion needs to be done after settlement of order or before settlement (KO8G).

While running settlement of order, what type of orders need to be selected out of in process, closed, technically completed, and released types?

✍ ANSWER

The standard procedure or flow is after TECO. You can then go for settlement afterwards.

So do the Release, confirmation and then TECO.

Technically speaking, you can perform settlement in either REL or TECO status.

Therefore it is up to your business or purpose to decide.

☞ QUESTION 92

Exits to validate item classification and notification data

We need to validate standard notification fields and also the data stored in the class characteristic field of notification at item level for updating a user status in service notification.

Can u suggest a suitable exit for this?

✍ ANSWER

You can investigate user-exit QQMA0014 (Checks before saving a notification).

An alternative solution can be as follows:

Get the classification (or maybe status) information into a user-exit.

You can also read the PROGRAM STACK in user-exits – and then ask your ABAP team.

☞ Question 93

Lube Routes

Can lube routes be created in SAP? I assume the best way is with an object list in the maintenance item.

If there is a better way, what is the process involved?

✍ Answer

There is an OSS Note to attach a measurement entry list to a maintenance plan. You can refer from it for guidance.

☞ QUESTION 94

Starting IW28, with variant, from a desktop icon

Currently I can create the icon but it only kicks off the transaction with the initial selection screen. I would like to be able to attach a variant to the icon and have it execute automatically so that the user would be presented with the appropriate list.

Is there a way to apply a selection variant to a desktop item created from the easy access menu?

✍ ANSWER

Try saving the variant as U_XXXXXX where XXXXXX as your user name.

Furthermore, if you add the display variant at the bottom of the selection-screen, then you can choose which fields to display.

This works for most of the PM list edit reports.

I noticed that this functionality is now creeping into other modules (MM and SD).

You can also add it to your own customer-specific ABAP reports. Get your ABAP guys to debug the initialization section of the program.

☞ Question 95

Maintenance work center mandatory in PM-order

At this moment the maintenance work center and planner group are mandatory fields in a PM01-order.

In the customizing (define field selection) I could only search for the planner group how this field is set mandatory for a certain order-type. However I couldn't find this setting for the maintenance work center.

Is this set a mandatory field? If so, how can I influence this?

✍ Answer

Check the influencing factors (button at the top of screen) in the field selection.

The main work center in the work order header is always mandatory, you can't change it.

In the initial screen, when you create a work order, enter a functional location which contains a work center. After this, you will not have a problem filling up this field.

☞ Question 96

Notification tabs are not showing

One time I copied the notification type M1 to create a new notification type. However, the reference object tab (equipment, functional location and assembly) is not showing in the new notification.

What is the reason for this?

✍ Answer

Ensure that you have tabs assigned to your notification type in the IMG (Set Screen Templates for the Notification Type).

Also make sure that the checkbox called Tab is set for each tab; this ensures that the tabs are displayed.

☞ QUESTION 97

Possibility to take over parameter after object change

Is it somehow possible that after a change of reference object, related data of the new reference object is automatically transferred into the order (E.G. related maintenance work center, planner group, settlement role etc)?

If I change the reference object, the system comes up with message 'IW501'.

"Object change ==> Order data might not be the same as default values
Message no. IW501"

Diagnosis
You changed the reference object of the maintenance order. However, certain data in the maintenance order refers to the original reference object.

The following data in particular is affected:

Settlement rule
Main work center
Assignment data of order header (for example, WBS element, business area)
Partner data
The delivery address for external resources derived from the reference object
System Response
The system does not change this default data automatically.

Procedure
Check whether the data of the maintenance order also applies to the new reference object and if necessary, change it.

How do I go about resolving this issue?

✍ ANSWER

Right-click with your mouse in the order, there should be an option for updating reference object data. From there, you may choose your options for resolving this.

Note: this option is usually not in the menu.

☞ QUESTION 98

Confirmation Data in Maintenance Plan Category

I don't want to set the Indicator in Confirmation Requirement at the time of maintenance plan creation.

What is the impact on Confirmation Data indicator in maintenance plan category?

✍ ANSWER

You can search for "Completion Requirement" procedures in the manual.

Essentially it means that if the box is checked, then the previous order (or other call object) must be TECOed before the next order is created.

Or an alternative approach would be:

When you TECO an order there is a reference date popup box, you will see two sets of dates/times (object and maintenance plan). This occurs when the confirmation data checkbox is set in the maintenance plan category. Otherwise there is only one set of dates/times.

See the field description below:

Indicator: Separate completion of maintenance call date;
You can use this indicator to influence the maintenance processing process. For example, you can prevent that every

employee who can complete orders and notifications can also influence the scheduling of maintenance plans through the data.

With this indicator you can:

1. Activate a separate completion for the maintenance plan for the completion of call object notification and order.

2. Activate a dialog for the completion of notifications and orders using list processing.

3. Activate additional functionality for completing the call objects notification and order using a BAdI.

☞ QUESTION 99

Use TCode 'cv01n' to upload one file to SAP

When I am using Tcode 'cv01n' to upload one file to sap and I click 'Check In'
button, it appears information 'SAP archiving for document type DOC maximum 0 bytes: file has 537,600 bytes'.

Can anyone tell me how to configure the maximum bytes?

✍ ANSWER

The transaction CV01N creates an object in SAP. This object is just a link with your document on your PC or on a server.

The transaction CV01N does not upload your file in SAP.

You can also check in transaction DC10 the value for 'file size'.

☞ QUESTION 100

Fleet Objects in 4.6c: TARE, GVM and GCM

We are currently putting together our design for fleet objects in 4.6c and are looking at the use of the fields for vehicle mass values.

Here are some acronyms:

Tare Weight: curb weight of the vehicle (including fuel and oils)
GVM: Gross Vehicle Mass
GCM: Gross Combined Mass (total mass of vehicle + mass of towed vehicle - as specified by the manufacturer)

What we've come up with (on the <Fleet 1> tab is:
Weight field --> Tare
Total Weight --> GVM
Max Load Weight --> GCM

The only issue we see with this is in transactions ie36 and ie37 where the 'Weight' field is reported as the 'Gross Weight'.

Are there any other issues that we should be aware of?

Are we better off using these fields in a different way? If so, what are our options?

✍ ANSWER

Here are two alternative options:

1. Use classification to include additional fields.
2. Utilize Enhancement ITOB0003 (Customer Include sub screen for fleet object data) to add the field and functionality.

INDEX

Attention SAP Experts

Have you ever considered writing a book in your area of SAP? Equity Press is the leading provider of knowledge products in SAP applications consulting, development, and support. If you have a manuscript or an idea of a manuscript, we'd love to help you get it published!

Please send your manuscript or manuscript ideas to jim@sapcookbook.com – we'll help you turn your dream into a reality.

Or mail your inquiries to:

Equity Press Manuscripts
BOX 706
Riverside, California
92502

Tel (951)788-0810
Fax (951)788-0812

50% Off your next SAPCOOKBOOK order

Interview books are great for cross-training

In the new global economy, the more you know the better. The sharpest consultants are doing everything they can to pick up more than one functional area of SAP. Each of the following Certification Review / Interview Question books provides an excellent starting point for your module learning and investigation. These books get you started like no other book can – by providing you the information that you really need to know, and fast.

SAPCOOKBOOK Interview Questions, Answers, and Explanations

ABAP -	SAP ABAP Certification Review: SAP ABAP Interview Questions, Answers, and Explanations
SD -	SAP SD Interview Questions, Answers, and Explanations
Security -	SAP Security: SAP Security Essentials
HR -	mySAP HR Interview Questions, Answers, and Explanations: SAP HR Certification Review
BW -	SAP BW Ultimate Interview Questions, Answers, and Explanations: SAW BW Certification Review
-	SAP SRM Interview Questions Answers and Explanations
Basis -	SAPBasisCertificationQuestions:BasisInterview Questions, Answers, and Explanations
MM -	SAP MM Certification and Interview Questions: SAP MM Interview Questions, Answers, and Explanations

SAP BW Ultimate Interview Questions, Answers, and Explanations

Key Topics Include:

- The most important BW settings to know
- BW tables and transaction code quick references
- Certification Examination Questions
- Extraction, Modeling and Configuration
- Transformations and Administration
- Performance Tuning, Tips & Tricks, and FAQ
- Everything a BW resource needs to know before an interview

mySAP HR Interview Questions, Answers, and Explanations

Key topics include:

- The most important HR settings to know
- mySAP HR Administration tables and transaction code quick references
- SAP HR Certification Examination Questions
- Org plan, Compensation, Year End, Wages, and Taxes
- User Management, Transport System, Patches, and Upgrades
- Benefits, Holidays, Payroll, and Infotypes
- Everything an HR resource needs to know before an interview

SAP SRM Interview Questions, Answers, and Explanations

Key Topics Include:

- The most important SRM Configuration to know
- Common EBP Implementation Scenarios
- Purchasing Document Approval Processes
- Supplier Self Registration and Self Service (SUS)
- Live Auctions and Bidding Engine, RFX Processes (LAC)
- Details for Business Intelligence and Spend Analysis
- EBP Technical and Troubleshooting Information

SAP MM Interview Questions, Answers, and Explanations

- The most important MM Configuration to know
- Common MM Implementation Scenarios
- MM Certification Exam Questions
- Consumption Based Planning
- Warehouse Management
- Material Master Creation and Planning
- Purchasing Document Inforecords

SAP SD Interview Questions, Answers, and Explanations

- The most important SD settings to know
- SAP SD administration tables and transaction code quick references
- SAP SD Certification Examination Questions
- Sales Organization and Document Flow Introduction
- Partner Procedures, Backorder Processing, Sales BOM
- Backorder Processing, Third Party Ordering, Rebates and Refunds
- Everything an SD resource needs to know before an interview

SAP Basis Interview Questions, Answers, and Explanations

- The most important Basis settings to know
- Basis Administration tables and transaction code quick references
- Certification Examination Questions
- Oracle database, UNIX, and MS Windows Technical Information
- User Management, Transport System, Patches, and Upgrades
- Backup and Restore, Archiving, Disaster Recover, and Security
- Everything a Basis resource needs to know before an interview

SAP Security Essentials

- Finding Audit Critical Combinations
- Authentication, Transaction Logging, and Passwords
- Roles, Profiles, and User Management
- ITAR, DCAA, DCMA, and Audit Requirements
- The most important security settings to know
- Security Tuning, Tips & Tricks, and FAQ
- Transaction code list and table name references

SAP Workflow Interview Questions, Answers, and Explanations

- Database Updates and Changing the Standard
- List Processing, Internal Tables, and ALV Grid Control
- Dialog Programming, ABAP Objects
- Data Transfer, Basis Administration
- ABAP Development reference updated for 2006!
- Everything an ABAP resource needs to know before an interview